CHOSEN JEWEL

STUDENT WORKBOOK

CHOSEN JEWEL

Copyright ©2019 by Caprice L. Lyons

All rights reserved. No part of this book may be reproduced, copied, stored or transmitted in any form or by any means – graphic, electronic, or mechanical, including photocopying, recording, or information storage and retrieval systems without the prior written permission of Caprice L. Lyons or HOV Publishing except where permitted by law.

Unless otherwise indicated, all Scriptures quotations are taken from The Holy Bible, The New International Version (NIV) Copyright 1973, 1978, 1984, 2011 by Biblica, Inc.
The NIV Study Bible (NIV) Copyright 1985, 1995, 2002, 2008, 2011
Published by Zondervan
3900 Sparks Dr., SE
Grand Rapids, Michigan 49546
www.zondervan.com. All rights reserved.

HOV Publishing a division of HOV, LLC.
www.hovpub.com
hopeofvision@gmail.com

Cover Design: HOV Design Solutions

Visit the Author Caprice L. Lyons at:
www.capricelyons.com
capricelyons@yahoo.com

For more information about special discounts for bulk purchases, please visit capricelyons@yahoo.com

ISBN 978-1-942871-52-1

10 9 8 7 6 5 4 3 2 1

Printed in the United States of America

TABLE OF CONTENTS

INTRODUCTION 1

CHOSEN JEWEL

CHAPTER 1 2

THE JEWEL OF LOVE - *Ruby*

CHAPTER 2 12

THE JEWEL OF FAITH - *Emerald*

CHAPTER 3 19

THE JEWEL OF CLARITY - *Topaz*

CHAPTER 4 24

THE JEWEL OF FLASHING - *Carbuncle*

CHAPTER 5 27

THE JEWEL OF ASPIRING - *Sapphire*

CHAPTER 6 32

THE JEWEL OF ENERGY & GROWTH - *Quartz*

CHAPTER 7 37

THE JEWEL OF WISDOM - *Jacinth*

CHAPTER 8 41

THE JEWEL OF BALANCE - *Agate*

CHAPTER 9 48

THE JEWEL OF HEALING - *Amethyst*

CHAPTER 10 52

THE JEWEL OF TRUTH - *Chrysotile*

CHAPTER 11 58

THE JEWEL OF POWER - *Onyx*

CHAPTER 12 64

THE JEWEL OF POSSIBILITIES - *Opal*

INTRODUCTION

~ Chosen Jewel ~

Thank you for making the decision to embark upon this journey of discovery. As you go through this study guide, you will have opportunities to reflect on your journey thus far. You may find that the Holy Spirit will bring things to the forefront of your consciousness that had long been buried away. You will be brought into a place where you will be challenged to examine the jewels in your life and learn the true value of each one. You will be led to explore how they have affected your walk and still exist to help you to come into the fullness of who God has designed you to be.

Using The Workbook

This study guide is best used in conjunction with my book entitled, <u>Chosen Jewel</u>. As you go through each chapter, it is quite possible that strong feelings may be brought to the surface. I encourage you to give the Holy Spirit permission to work in you to bring healing and deliverance. Your life is about to change for the better!

Although we have provided writing space in the workbook, you may need an additional notepad, as well as a highlighter. You may also feel the need to begin a journal as the Holy Spirit brings clarity to things that have happened in your own life. Most importantly, make sure you have access to a good Bible for scriptural references as you go through the lessons.

Chapter 1: *Jewel of Love*

Ruby

I.   Ruby is an _____.

_____

_____

_____

_____

_____

_____

II.   Love is a force of _____. It cannot be

1. _____

_____

_____

_____

2. _____

_____

_____

_____

CHAPTER 1: JEWEL OF LOVE

3. _____

_____

_____

_____

III. The Lord our God was the first one to share this precious gift of love.

_____

_____

_____

IV. The love that God shares is the purest form of love.

So, many things are represented in the earth by love, but nothing can compare to the example that God has given us. Quite often, when we think about love, we think of loving others in a caring way and in some cases, in an intimate way.

_____

_____

_____

V. Loving _____ is an important part of being able to love _____, as well as being able to love _____.

_____

_____

_____

CHAPTER 1: JEWEL OF LOVE

VI. The lack of love in the world is a _____, yet _____ problem, because the enemy wants to cast blame on people and have them at odds with each other.

VII. The lack of love is the cause of many issues such as:

- _____
- _____
- _____
- _____
- _____
- _____

_____
_____
_____

VIII. When you truly love _____, you love who you are and _____ the _____ that you have done.

1. _____ of the wrong is not _____ of the wrong. Wrong is wrong and it will always be wrong.
2. It is very important that you know the difference between _____ and _____ and that you are willing to _____ The things that you did so that you can move forward in your life, and into a _____ and _____ place with yourself.

_____
_____
_____

CHAPTER 1: JEWEL OF LOVE

3. Where you _____, 'you' _____.

   _____
   _____
   _____

4. The process of _____ involves

   - _____ your wrongs
   - _____ yourself
   - _____ anything that you can if it is possible.

   _____
   _____
   _____

5. You will have to put the work in daily to change old _____ and _____, it will not be easy, but it will be worth it.

   _____
   _____
   _____

IX. The devil is _____.

A. He _____ your _____.

   _____
   _____
   _____

   1. He puts _____ in your way so that you feel that there is no other way out. Very often the _____ comes, but it may not be enough to stop the cycle.

   _____

CHAPTER 1: JEWEL OF LOVE

_____

_____

B. In John 10:10, we read that "The thief comes to steal and kill and destroy; I have come that they may have life and have it to the full."

_____

_____

_____

_____

X. **When you _____ yourself, you are more likely to make the right _____ for all the right _____.**

_____

_____

_____

_____

XI. **The light from our Jewel will be so _____ in the presence of others that they may see it before we even know that it is there.**

_____

_____

1. When you deal with people long enough you just know certain things about their character without much conversation or interaction with them.

_____

_____

CHAPTER 1: JEWEL OF LOVE

2. First impressions are lasting impressions.

   _____

   _____

3. Make sure that your first impression is a good one and that you carry yourself like you want to be perceived.

   _____

   _____

XII. The most needed component for moving forward is _____.

1. Until we _____ ourselves, we are good for no one.
2. If we don't believe in _____, we cannot _____.
3. If we don't believe we can be _____, we will not be _____.
4. If we have unhealthy stipulations about _____, it will be hard for someone to _____ us.

   _____

   _____

   A. Love will enable each of us to be like a _____ that is drawn to others who know how to love correctly.

   B. Our _____ can begin when we accept that we are not alone in the struggle, and we learn how to love _____ and _____.

   C. It is vital that we overcome hurt or betrayal through _____ and _____ no matter whose fault it was.

   _____

   _____

   _____

   _____

CHAPTER 1: JEWEL OF LOVE

XIII. The _____ inside of you are always calling you to a better place.

1. You must love yourself enough to _____ the feeling inside of you and to trust _____,

_____
_____

XIV. God knows what will bring about a _____ in your life.

1. There is a price to pay for your _____. You will appreciate everything thing that you do and get when God begins to reteach and restore to you.

_____
_____
_____

The apartment that I stayed in, where I obtained all my illegal drug possessions, burned to the ground when the couple living next door got into a fight. When God started me over, I could not take all that corruptible stuff with me. He started me with a firm foundation and I got more with Him than I had selling drugs. I got saved nine months later. Even though my turn-around had to be a crash and burn, God knew what it took to get my attention. If you are at a turn-around point, or in the midst of a crash and burn, there is life after.

XV. _____ has a way of burying itself and it will hide itself deep until it exposes itself.

_____
_____

CHAPTER 1: JEWEL OF LOVE

XVI. _____, _____, and _____ tries to take over everything good or anything with _____.

_____

_____

XVII. _____ will show up in our good places.

_____

_____

1. Unresolved issues will not _____ unless we do the work to _____ them.

_____

_____

2. Unresolved issues come with lots of _____, feelings of _____, and _____ that Will make us feel like that is who we are.

_____

_____

XVIII. It is the _____ of _____ that will:

1. Keep us in the _____ place.

_____

_____

2. Calm us and change our _____.

_____

_____

A. We must never allow _____ to define our _____.

_____

CHOSEN JEWEL WORKBOOK

CHAPTER 1: JEWEL OF LOVE

XIX. Learning to love yourself means embracing the past, present and future.

1. You must accept who you _____.

_____

_____

2. You must accept who you _____.

_____

_____

3. You must accept who you _____.

_____

_____

"Who you were, who you are, and who you will be are three different people."
~author unknown

XX. Fail to embrace love will keep you in _____.

1. You will spend everyday reliving the old _____, _____, and _____.

_____

_____

You MUST make the choice to be FREE today!!!

CHAPTER 1: JEWEL OF LOVE

XXI. It is love that makes the jewels in us so _____.

1. We must know how to:
   - _____ love.
   - _____ love.
   - _____ love.
   - _____ love.
   - _____ love.

_____
_____
_____

XXII. Women are creatures who are _____. To nurture is to _____ and _____, as during the period of training or development; _____ to: feed and _____; to bring up; _____ and _____.

1. To nurture is to _____.
2. Above all guard your heart (where your love is stored) for it determines the course of your life. (Proverbs 4:23 NLT).

   Maintain this Love Jewel at all costs; everything you do flows from it. The Love Jewel is the essence of who you are and it controls your ability to function. If love is not stored and nurtured correctly, it can lead to many dysfunctions.

_____
_____
_____

CHAPTER 2: JEWEL OF FAITH

CHAPTER 2: *JEWEL OF FAITH*

Emerald

I. **Emerald is the _____.**

_____

_____

_____

_____

_____

_____

II. **Faith is defined as belief with strong convictions; firm belief in something for which there may be _____; complete trust, confidence, reliance or devotion.**

   1. Faith is the opposite of _____. Hebrew 11:1 (KJV) states, *"Now faith is the substance of things hoped for, the evidence of things not seen."*

   _____

   _____

   _____

   _____

CHOSEN JEWEL WORKBOOK 12

CHAPTER 2: JEWEL OF FAITH

2. Although everyone wants more faith, oftentimes we want the faith without going through the _____ necessary to _____ it.

   _____
   _____
   _____
   _____

3. Everyone has faith for certain things. (cf. Rom.12:3b)

   _____
   _____
   _____
   _____

4. We can have more faith in some areas than others because we have used that _____ to believe for more and we saw the _____ of our _____, which made it easier.

   _____
   _____
   _____
   _____

5. Believing God for a new thing, requires new faith.

   _____
   _____
   _____
   _____

CHAPTER 2: JEWEL OF FAITH

6. _____, faith does not solve uncertainty and does not give answers to every question.

   _____
   _____
   _____
   _____

7. The uncertainty of faith enhances our senses to be aware of _____, _____, and _____.

   _____
   _____
   _____

III. **The jewels inside of you are activated by the call of God upon your life.**

   _____
   _____
   _____

   1. There is a _____ factor that always works in _ to the will of God for your life.

      _____
      _____

      A. The enemy puts _____ jewels in our life hoping to blind us so that we will see differently about ourselves our lives.

      B. Synthetic jewels are designed to _____ you so that you lose focus of your destiny.

CHAPTER 2: JEWEL OF FAITH

_____

_____

_____

IV. Your relationship with God is a personal thing.

1. Do not base it on the fact that you may be a little 'rough around the edges'.

_____

_____

2. Do not base it on someone else's relationship with Him.

_____

_____

3. Do not base it on what someone else says.

_____

_____

V. God works in our _____.

1. When God shows up in our situations, the encounter that we have with Him will be one that changes our perspective about who we are and where we are going.

   A. We must be able to _____ it so that we don't miss the opportunities.

   _____

   _____

   _____

CHAPTER 2: JEWEL OF FAITH

B. On the way through transition, God will honor your prayers.

_____
_____
_____
_____

C. Faith is required in the transition.

When you have faith about something in your life, there will be a time when changes will have to be made in the things you do and in your relationships with people. It does not matter whether it is having faith for a business, a spouse, a promotion, children or a scholarship.

_____
_____
_____
_____

D. Faith will come at a price. The price depends on where we are and what the call is on each of our lives.

_____
_____
_____
_____

2. During the transition, we have to free ourselves from _____.
John 4:1-30 can be summarized by saying, just like the Samaritan woman at the well, the disciples were with Jesus on His journey. But when He went to the well, the disciples were not with Him, they went to go get food. Jesus had His conversation with her in private. God does not need an audience when He deals with us.

_____
_____

CHAPTER 2: JEWEL OF FAITH

_____

_____

A. When God is giving us revelation and direction it is not the time to second guess Him and ask someone else what they think about what He said.

_____

_____

_____

_____

B. Changing, or un-changing, takes work.

_____

_____

_____

_____

VI. Faith is important because:

1. It is the lifeline that gets us from one dream to another, and from one destination to another.
2. It gives us a boost when things seem like they are not going to work out.
3. It keeps dreams alive.
4. It helps us when people we love have a problem with who we are becoming and with our progress.
5. Faith moves mountains.

Matthew 17:20 says, "He replied, "Because you have so little faith. Truly I tell you, if you have faith as small as a mustard seed, you can say to this mountain, 'Move from here to there,' and it will move. Nothing will be impossible for you." (NIV)

CHAPTER 2: JEWEL OF FAITH

_____
_____
_____
_____
_____
_____
_____
_____
_____
_____

CHAPTER 3: *JEWEL OF CLARITY*

I. Topez is a _____ and _____ stone.

    A. It balances emotions.

    B. It releases tension.

    C. It can bring joy.

_____

_____

_____

_____

II. _____: the equality or state of being clear; the quality of being easily understood; the equality of being easily seen or head.

    1. Clarity has a powerful influence over our thoughts process and how we comprehend things.

    2. We must have a clarity in our mind to make sound decisions.

    3. We need a clear mind to be free.

_____

_____

_____

CHAPTER 3: JEWEL OF CLARITY

1 Peter 5:8 says, *"Be alert and of sober mind. Your enemy the devil prowls around like a roaring lion looking for someone to devour."* 1 Peter 1:13 also says, *"Therefore, with minds that are alert and fully sober, set your hope on the grace to be brought to you when Jesus Christ is revealed at His coming."* James 1:8 says, *"He is a double-minded man, unstable in all his ways."*

_____
_____
_____
_____

4. Clarity will allow us to take ownership in what we have done in our lives.

_____
_____
_____
_____

5. Clarity is very important to get you to the next place in your life.
    A. If we are going through something that is taking our clarity, God will stay the hand of the enemy so that we can make a conscious decision to ask for help.

_____
_____
_____
_____

III. **Make up your mind to embrace clarity and be crystal clear about every aspect of who you are, and who you are not.**

CHAPTER 3: JEWEL OF CLARITY

1. The enemy will use our insecurities and shame to push us away from something good and positive.
2. Satan will use our familiarity with people to hold us hostage in an environment that is only destroying the person that we are meant to be.
3. Just as we can't allow our negative feelings to keep us in a place because we are comfortable, we can't allow the feelings that make us feel uncomfortable in a positive place make us run.

_____

_____

_____

_____

IV. Your relationship with God is a personal thing.

1. We must think clearly about:
   - what our goals are
   - what our next steps will be
   - what short-term changes we can make
   - what long-term changes we can plan for

2. The best way to see with clarity is through eyes that give us a clear, honest view of who we are.

_____

_____

_____

_____

V. A desire for clarity sometimes demands that we _____ ourselves.

CHAPTER 3: JEWEL OF CLARITY

Matthew 12:43-45 says, *"When an impure spirit comes out of a person, it goes through arid places seeking rest and does not find it. Then it says, 'I will return to the house I left.' When it arrives, it finds the house unoccupied, swept clean and put in order. Then it goes and takes with it seven other spirits more wicked than itself, and they go in and live there. And the final condition of that person is worse than the first. That is how it will be with this wicked generation."*

We all need human connections in life. However, we should make sure that we choose the correct connections and that we are doing the right things to have those connections.

1. It is very important as we start growing and learning that we don't revert to those diluted behaviors when others are not able to accept who we are becoming.
2. Our differences may scare people; they may not accept the new us. Not because they don't want better for us, but they may be afraid of where they will fit in, or they may not want to face the changes that they need to make in their lives in order to stay connected to the new us.

_____

_____

_____

_____

VI. There are two options for our view of the Jewel of Clarity. They are our _____ and our _____.

1. We use our mind to _____.
2. We use our eyes to _____.

_____

_____

CHOSEN JEWEL WORKBOOK

CHAPTER 3: JEWEL OF CLARITY

_____

_____

We think clearly of what we want and where we want to be, and then we see ourselves there. Clarity will allow us to chase after the vision and the path will be clear. It's time to run for it!

CHAPTER 4: *JEWEL OF FLASHING*

CHAPTER 4: *JEWEL OF FLASHING*

Carbuncle

I. **Carbuncle: In Isaiah 54:12, the Hebrew word is '*ekdah*, used in the prophetic description of the glory and beauty of the mansions above.**

_____

_____

1. Next to the diamond, it is the hardest and most costly of all precious stones.

   _____

   _____

2. Flash: to shine or give off bright suddenly or in repeated burst; to appear quickly or suddenly; to move or pass very quickly.

   _____

   _____

   A. The enemy's job is to keep us moving so fast that we don't observe our surroundings. We don't use good reasoning and we do not pay attention to details. God wants us to be still and know that He is God. God is aware of all things. It is our reaction that is the catalyst in the situation.

   _____

CHAPTER 4: JEWEL OF FLASHING

_____

B. When life becomes too overwhelming, take the time to remember the moments when flashes of lifelines come to help pull you out of tough situations, or when lifelines keep you from making mistakes that can be avoided.

_____

_____

C. We have to take the time to reflect on our day and our life so that when things in life happen, we don't lose ourselves in folly when we know who God is and what He has done.

_____

_____

D. People will show us flashes or glimpses of who they are. Do not ignore the flashes. People's character shows who they are all the time and we do not want to overlook or give excuses for behavior that is not good for us.

_____

_____

II. The Jewel of Flash is _____.

1. It is a moment in time where there is an opportunity to get valuable knowledge that will get us closer to answers that we have been wanting.

_____

_____

2. These moments are nuggets in time
   A. Listen to them.
   B. Understand their meanings.

_____

CHAPTER 4: JEWEL OF FLASHING

_____

3. The Jewel is in the Flash.

_____

_____

III. **The Jewel of Flash is connected to** _____.

1. We have to understand the connection of what is going on at that time and what the Flash is trying to tell us.

_____

_____

Chapter 5: *Jewel of Aspiring*

I. Sapphire is a stone of _____, and _____, of _____ and Divine _____.

_____
_____

II. The Aspire: to want to have or achieve something (such as a particular career or level of success); to seek to attain or accomplish a particular goal.

_____
_____

III. We can limit who, where, and what we can be if we don't allow women who are beautiful and powerful to inspire us.

How much sense does it make to not take wisdom from someone who is intelligent and keeps her appearance together because you are insecure? If that is a hang-up for us it needs to change. That is an immature thought process.

_____
_____

CHAPTER 5: JEWEL OF ASPIRING

    1. We can't allow our feelings to cause us to miss out on information that could change our situation.

    _____

    _____

    2. Give other women their props and acknowledge what they can teach us, how they look, and their accomplishments.

    _____

    _____

IV.   Aspire: to want to have or achieve something (such as a particular career or level of success); to seek to attain or accomplish a particular goal.

    _____

    _____

    1. Aspiring and empowering other women is for us to have part in another woman's valve.

        A. Ownership in this sense means an _____.

    _____

    _____

V.   As women, we are _____.

    _____

    _____

    1. Extravagant is defined as excessively high; exceeding the bounds of reason, as actions demands, opinions or passions; beyond what is deserved or justifiable.

    _____

    _____

CHAPTER 5: JEWEL OF ASPIRING

VI. Behaviors that Affect our Female Relationships

1. The _____ woman

   A. She has wrong motives.

   B. She is plotting our demise and trying to get close to us, so she can destroy and infect everything that we are working on.

   _____
   _____
   _____
   _____

2. Low _____ for growth

   A. Some women's capacity cannot withstand the growth of others—even their friends.

   _____
   _____
   _____
   _____

   i. If the situation is unhealthy, by all means, move, but continue to pray and hold that position in your friendship.

   _____
   _____

   ii. If the enemy gets you to move out of your position, then her purpose and your purpose can be delayed. The right thing to do is to bring women up as you come up. God is watching.

   _____
   _____

CHAPTER 5: JEWEL OF ASPIRING

3. Sometimes when women become successful they forget about people who were with them back when things were tough.

_____
_____
_____
_____

   A. While it may be necessary to change your constellation, remember to be prayerful before doing so.

_____
_____
_____
_____

VII. The Benefits of "True" Friendship

1. True friends are _____ in their dealings with each other.

_____
_____
_____
_____

2. Friends _____, _____, and _____ each other.

_____
_____
_____
_____

CHAPTER 5: JEWEL OF ASPIRING

3. There is an even _____ in a giving relationship.

_____

_____

_____

_____

4. True friends are _____ to each other.

_____

_____

_____

_____

CHAPTER 6: *JEWEL OF ENERGY, GROWTH*

Quartz Crystal

I. **Quartz enhances _____, _____ and _____.**

_____

_____

II. **_____: a stage in the process of growing: full growth; progressive development; increase, expansion; maturing; a natural process of increasing in size or developing; a gradual increase; something producing and growing.**

_____

_____

_____

_____

III. **_____: God promises to stay involved through the lifelong process of spiritual growth.**

Philippians 1:6 states, *"...being confident of this very thing, that He who has begun a good work in you will complete it until the day of Jesus Christ."* You have to stay connected with Jesus. In life, you have to stay connected with the right people.

_____

CHAPTER 6: JEWEL OF ENERGY, GROWTH

_____
_____
_____

1. We While moving forward, whether our steps are fast or slow, make sure that there is growth.

_____
_____

2. Growth is a part of God's _____.

_____
_____

3. Growth is set up on _____ that have to be followed in ordered for them to work, and at any given stage, the growth can be stunted if something is skipped.

_____
_____

    i. Every day that we get up, we are going to school at _____.

_____
_____

    ii. The cost is our _____.

_____
_____

    iii. The _____ of our survival is up to us

_____
_____

CHAPTER 6: JEWEL OF ENERGY, GROWTH

a. If we are not living life well, we may experience such symptoms and/or emotions such as:
- Feeling down
- Depression
- Crying
- Calling out for help
- Searching for something that is missing

_____
_____
_____
_____

4. Growth takes _____.

_____
_____

i. A woman who is _____ in her growth, is a woman of _____.

_____
_____
_____
_____

IV. **Be careful who you _____ to. Spirits and behaviors _____.**

_____
_____
_____
_____

CHAPTER 6: JEWEL OF ENERGY, GROWTH

1. Having the right kind of people around us is very important.

   _____
   _____
   _____
   _____
   _____

2. Connecting with productive women will generate the right energy and cause us to plunge ourselves into places we may not normally go because our energy was not wasted.

   _____
   _____
   _____
   _____
   _____

3. Pray that God places women full of positive energy in your circle.

   _____
   _____
   _____
   _____
   _____

V. **It is important to make the right _____.**

   _____
   _____
   _____
   _____
   _____

CHAPTER 6: JEWEL OF ENERGY, GROWTH

VI. There are 3 levels of choices.

1. *Level 1:* Choosing _____ over _____.

   _____

   _____

   _____

   _____

2. *Level 2:* Choosing _____ over _____ and _____ over _____.

   _____

   _____

   _____

   _____

3. *Level 3:* Choosing _____ for _____.

   _____

   _____

   _____

   _____

CHAPTER 7: JEWEL OF WISDOM

Jacinth

I. Jacinth is the _____ of _____.

_____
_____

A. The virtue is able to impart _____ to the _____ as well as the _____.

_____
_____

II. _____: ability to discern inner qualities and relationships; good sense; knowledge that is gained by having many experiences in life.

_____
_____
_____
_____

III. _____. (I Kings 3:5-15)

_____
_____
_____

CHAPTER 7: JEWEL OF WISDOM

1. When you become enlightened to wisdom it will take you to another level of _____.

   _____

   _____

2. _____ will allow us to stand strong no matter what we have been through.

   _____

   _____

3. Wisdom lets us know that we are _____ by God.

   _____

   _____

4. Wisdom will remind us and allow us to _____ on the things that caused us pain or hindered us in life. Proverbs 4:6 says *"Do not forsake wisdom, and she will protect you; love her, and she will watch over you. The beginning of wisdom in this: Get wisdom. Though it cost all you have, get understanding."*

   _____

   _____

5. Wisdom will stand guard to _____ us by giving us instructions on how to avoid dangerous pitfalls.

   _____

   _____

6. Wisdom should be so loud that when the old foolishness shows up, we should be moving in the other direction.

   _____

   _____

CHAPTER 7: JEWEL OF WISDOM

A. If you are falling for the same sins, setbacks, downfalls, or into the same pits, it is time to do _____. You may not be able to do the evaluation on yourself; you might need to get help.

    i. The worst thing is to get others tied up in our mess knowing we are not ready to change. People are willing to help us, but we must be sincere in our request.

_____
_____

    ii. We have to be able to carry our own weight at some point. We cannot be victims all our lives, needing assistance in everything we do.

_____
_____

    iii. Wanting _____ vs. wanting _____

_____
_____

7. Wisdom is _____.

_____
_____
_____

    A. It covers the _____ and the _____.

_____
_____

8. When making _____, we have to think and wait on wisdom to help us make the right choices.

CHAPTER 7: JEWEL OF WISDOM

_____

_____

_____

_____

9. _____ wisdom when she shows up. _____
   The truth about what she tells you because wisdom can be your best friend. (Proverbs 4:5-7)

_____

_____

_____

_____

IV. Wisdom is the _____ of all the Jewels because wisdom knows what the other Jewels don't know.

_____

_____

_____

_____

_____

_____

_____

CHAPTER 8: *JEWEL OF BALANCE*

Agate

I. **Agate promotes _____, _____, and _____.**

   A. Its warm, protective properties encourage _____ and _____.

   _____
   _____
   _____
   _____

II. **Balance: the ability to move or to remain in a position without losing control or falling; a state in which different things occur in equal or proper amounts or have an equal or proper amount of importance.**

   _____
   _____
   _____
   _____

III. **Balance is the center of things. _____ is the part of your balance system that provides your brain with information about changes in head movement with respect to the pull of gravity.**

CHAPTER 8: JEWEL OF BALANCE

_____
_____
_____
_____

1. Balance is one of the key factors to _____ or _____.

_____
_____

2. Balance is for _____.

_____
_____

3. There is _____ for balance in your life.

_____
_____

   A. Being _____ causes so many underlying issues that will leave important things overlooked.

   _____
   _____
   _____
   _____

   B. Being unbalanced causes issues, whatever is _____ or whatever _____, to take precedence over everything.

   _____
   _____
   _____
   _____

CHAPTER 8: JEWEL OF BALANCE

IV. _____ balance makes way for the devil to operate and cause _____ in our life.

    1. Our mindset will trap us into poor _____ and _____.

          i. Before we know it, our lack of attention will cause us to forget things that are important and cause us to focus on things that are not productive.

    2. We must remember to balance both the big and the small things in our lives.

V. **Balance requires _____.**

    1. We have to be attuned to when we are vulnerable so that we stay self-controlled.

VI. **Let's win _____!**

CHAPTER 8: JEWEL OF BALANCE

_____

_____

1. We should make sure that our balance is strong and level so that our wins are good wins.

   _____

   _____

2. From the perspective of the quality of the win, we should make sure that our balance is strong and level so that our wins are good wins.

   _____

   _____

3. We Let's take advantage of experience and education and not just slide in, or barely make it in.

   _____

   _____

VII. **The quality of our _____ is just as important as the _____.**

_____

_____

_____

1. We need to have a perspective that will allow us to see beyond the loss or disappointment.

   _____

   _____

2. Hopefully, we will understand the loss and be better prepared the next Time.

CHOSEN JEWEL WORKBOOK 44

CHAPTER 8: JEWEL OF BALANCE

_____

_____

   3. We have to be able to take a loss and be functional.

_____

_____

       A. _____ is a loss that can impair and can kill us if we are in a vulnerable place.

_____

_____

VIII. **_____ is not a part of balance.**

_____

_____

_____

_____

   1. You must have balance of _____ you are and _____ you are.

_____

_____

   2. Balance cannot _____.

_____

_____

   3. Balance will always leave the _____ in awe.

_____

_____

CHAPTER 8: JEWEL OF BALANCE

    4. Balance is aligning our _____ with _____.

_____
_____
_____

IX. We must understand that we can be in the _____ of God and all hell can still break loose.

    1. We have to know who God is.

_____
_____

    2. We must understand that God is building something that will be able to stay balanced throughout any attack, test, or challenge.

_____
_____

When we encounter mishap after mishap or when life seems unfair, we cannot allow ourselves or people to make us think that we have sinned, and we are not in right- standing with God. God is in His creative mode and He will work out everything for our good.

X. When things align with balance, _____ will not seem to be impossible or overwhelming.

_____
_____
_____
_____

CHAPTER 8: JEWEL OF BALANCE

XI. Balance allows for _____ and gives a plan to accomplish great things and win.

_____

_____

_____

_____

If loss happens, the Jewel of Balance gives nuggets that turn it into a positive loss.

CHAPTER 9: JEWEL OF HEALING

I. _____ is based on the stone's ancient reputation for preventing _____, which was perhaps sympathetic magic suggested by its wine like color.

_____
_____
_____
_____

II. _____: to make healthy, whole, or sound; restore to health; free from ailment; to bring to an end or conclusion, as conflicts between people or groups, usually with the strong implication of restoring former amity; settle; reconcile; to free from evil; cleanse; purify.

_____
_____
_____
_____

1. When we are being healed there will be times when we will have to move like a _____ and change with the situation.

   Something happened but we still have to move as if nothing has happened, changing and blending-in with the scenery as we go. We all go

CHAPTER 9: JEWEL OF HEALING

through things, but we cannot allow those things to incapacitate us. We have to keep moving through it.

_____
_____

2. When we are healed it is an announcement to our inner selves, as well as to the enemy and the world.

_____
_____

3. We have to own our healing; it is a _____.

_____
_____

4. Being healed is to learn to _____ ourselves because we are not our own enemy. However, if we _____ ourselves long enough we can turn on ourselves and begin to think we are the enemy.

_____
_____

   A. Sometimes we spend a lot of time battling _____.

   _____
   _____

   B. We have to be healed from that old "self" and walk in our new self.

   _____
   _____

III. **We have to be alright with the seasons when we do not fit in, these are _____ and _____ seasons.**

_____
_____
_____

CHAPTER 9: JEWEL OF HEALING

IV. **When things happen in our lives that we have done to ourselves or if others have done it to us, our body will go into healing mode.**

_____

_____

_____

_____

1. The thing that keeps us from healing is,_____.
   If we relive the events and keep talking about them that keeps the pain open and fresh and prevents the healing process.

   _____

   _____

V. **The body is made to repair itself but if we keep_____ it, the body will go into _____.**

_____

_____

_____

_____

1. If left untreated, shock is usually fatal, but it can be treated depending on the cause.

   _____

   _____

2. Our shock may not literally kill us, but it can kill the healing process that enables us to have a productive life for ourselves, our families, and our destiny.

_____

_____

VI. The Jewel of Healing is _____ to the body that fights off any imbalances and anything that goes against God's perfect will for our life.

_____

_____

Chapter 10: Jewel of Truth

Chrysolite

I. Chrysolite is also known as _____. It is the stone of

- _____
- _____
- _____

_____
_____
_____
_____

II. Truth: the real facts about something; the things that are true; the quality or state of being true; a statement or idea that is true or accepted as true.

_____
_____
_____
_____

III. Your _____ should be what God thinks.

1. Don't let people write your future for you based on their assumptions or your past.

CHAPTER 10: JEWEL OF TRUTH

_____

_____

2. Don't write your future based on your past, or what you think.

_____

_____

IV. _____ is sometimes the _____

That will allow dreams, purpose, and destiny to grow.

1. Sometimes you need to _____.
2. Sometimes you need to _____.
   It's okay!

_____

_____

1. If we struggle with doubt or have genuine questions, we shouldn't panic or feel reluctant to seek the truth. God will meet us, and faith will spring from the answers we find.

_____

_____

2. If we are sincerely looking for answers, God will meet us, and faith will spring from the answers we find.

_____

_____

3. There will be some questions that we will not get the answers for in this lifetime. Keep pursuing righteousness and everything will work out.

_____

_____

CHAPTER 10: JEWEL OF TRUTH

V. **In order to be successful, we have to know who we are.**

1. When we know who we are:

    1. Our success will take sacrifice and hard work.

        _____

        _____

    2. It will require us to be resolved in our mind so that we will be true to who we are, no matter what.

        _____

        _____

    3. We will have to understand what type of person we want to be.

        _____

        _____

        Many people are true to themselves, but they are not the most honest, sincere, or loveable people, and they are okay with that. We have to know what type of person we want to be and stick to it.

    4. The ultimate test to see if we are really true to ourselves is to reflect on our response when someone says or does something wrong to us.

        _____

        _____

In 1 Peter 3:15, it says, *"But in your hearts revere Christ as Lord. Always be prepared to give an answer to everyone who asks you to give the reason for the hope that you have. But do this with gentleness and respect, keeping a clear conscience, so that those who speak maliciously against your good behavior in Christ may be ashamed of their slander. For it is better, if it is God's will, to suffer for doing good than for doing evil."* Your hope is to please God and to show the world there is a higher power that works in you.

CHAPTER 10: JEWEL OF TRUTH

5. The We have to be so true with ourselves, about ourselves, and what we did, because:

   A. People in their ignorance, insecurities, or efforts to be hurtful and destroy our progress will do and say things to cause our setback.

   _____

   _____

   B. Sometimes people are genuine in wanting to know how we were able to conquer such a big giant. The thing that we went through may have been tough for them.

   _____

   _____

   C. A friend or loved one may need our knowledge, so they can help themselves or someone else.

   _____

   _____

VI. We say we want truth, but

1. Are we willing to see the reflection of ourselves regardless of our feelings?
2. Are we willing to pay the price?
3. Are we willing to accept 100% responsibility for truth about who we are, be it good or bad?
4. Are we willing to get the counseling or mentoring that we may need to overcome things that are hindering us?

_____

_____

_____

_____

CHAPTER 10: JEWEL OF TRUTH

VII. In order to be successful, we have to know who we are.

1. When we know who we are, our success will take sacrifice and hard work.
2. It will require us to be resolved in our mind so that we will be true to who we are, no matter what.
3. We will have to understand what type of person we want to be.

   A. Many people are true to themselves, but they are not the most honest, sincere, or loveable people, and they are okay with that.
   B. The ultimate test to see if we are really true to ourselves is to reflect on our response when someone says or does something wrong to us. Will we stay true to our genuine self? Will we still be that loving caring person? We all know when the right buttons are pushed how we can react.

   _____

   _____

   In 1 Peter 3:15, it says, *"But in your hearts revere Christ as Lord. Always be prepared to give an answer to everyone who asks you to give the reason for the hope that you have. But do this with gentleness and respect, keeping a clear conscience, so that those who speak maliciously against your good behavior in Christ may be ashamed of their slander. For it is better, if it is God's will, to suffer for doing good than for doing evil."*

VIII. If we don't face our truth. The enemy will attempt to use it against us.

1. Facing our truth may prevent posterity from walking the same painful path we did.
2. We have to be so true with ourselves, about ourselves, and what we did, because people in their ignorance, insecurities, or efforts to be hurtful and destructive to our progress will do and say things to cause our

CHAPTER 10: JEWEL OF TRUTH

setback.

_____
_____
_____
_____

IX. **If Being offended and taking things personally can hurt our victory and our freedom.**

1. When people ask us about our past and our deliverance, we have to be confident in our answers and reactions.

   _____
   _____
   _____
   _____

2. Don't be so caught up in trying to figure out everyone's motives.

   _____
   _____
   _____
   _____

3. The only thing that will hold us in a place of falsehood and shame is giving the power to the enemy and allowing him to hold the truth.

   _____
   _____
   _____
   _____

Chapter 11: *Jewel of Power*

I. Onyx is thought to have protective properties and to bring inner _____, self-confidence and mental _____, will _____.

_____

_____

_____

_____

II. _____: having great power, prestige, or influence; leading to many or important deductions; having the ability to control or influence people or things; having a strong effect on someone or something; having or producing a lot of physical strength or force.

III. How a person _____, _____, or _____ for themselves reflects how they receive their order.

_____

_____

_____

CHAPTER 11: JEWEL OF POWER

When you are in this walk called life, there will be times when you have special orders that you want from God and out of life, you will have to decide out of the three how you will receive your order.

1. The Order, Pull Up, Grab, and Go is called _____.
2. The Order, Pull Up, Check, and Go is called _____.
3. The Order, Pull Up, and Wait is called _____.

_____
_____
_____
_____

1. _____

Have you ever been deceived? Not that God is a Man that He should lie and not give us what we ask or desired, but there is another force at work here in the earth and that is the enemy.

   A. The enemy's job is to _____ anything that God is doing in our life.

   _____
   _____

   B. The wonderful things about God is that He will give us _____ for our _____.

   _____
   _____

   He knows the length of our wait, the sacrifice, our patience, the desire of our heart, and the faith that it took for us to stay in line to receive the order.

   _____
   _____

CHAPTER 11: JEWEL OF POWER

    C. 'I'll Take Whatever' seems quick but it can be _____.

_____

_____

2. _____

   If we have prayed, planned, or saved for something that we have wanted a long time and we waited for it, that has become our _____. We didn't get other things because we wanted this _____ thing. We planned for it and it took time for us to wait it out.

_____

_____

_____

    A. There can be so many things happening at one time that we can lose _____ of the details of what we want.

_____

_____

    B. _____ is checking with God to make sure that this is the right move to make.

_____

_____

3. _____

    A. You will have to determine the _____ of your order.

_____

_____

    B. Everybody's wait is not the same.

_____

_____

CHAPTER 11: JEWEL OF POWER

We will need line checkers to pray with us even if they may not understand the passion that we have for our wait, but they believe that God will be God and that His will be done in our lives.

IV. The _____

This decision can make or break a situation and it can determine the timeframe in which we receive our _____.

_____

_____

If we have paid the price through our tests, trials, and persecution and God promised us something, we should not forfeit because we don't want to wait.

_____

_____

Would you go in a furniture store and pick out what you want, pay for it, and then leave it because they took too long putting it on the truck? If you paid for something it is yours.

When we ask God for something and it does not happen right then, He is saying, "Yes, but <u>wait</u>."

_____

_____

1. _____ is a part of the _____.

_____

_____

2. If we would only trust God enough to know that He can do it, we will have the courage to _____.

_____

_____

CHAPTER 11: JEWEL OF POWER

3. You will be counted _____ because you believed?

   _____
   _____

   Genesis 22:1-14 says, *"Abraham was counted faithful."* God told Abraham to take his only son to sacrifice him. Abraham left the servants, he knew if he took the servants with them to build the altar he would have to do too much talking about the sacrifice and what God told him to do. He told them to stay there and await his return. Abraham had an expectation, do you?

4. Having realistic standards is being _____.

   _____
   _____

5. When we come into the knowledge of the Jewels that we possess, we learn to not just settle for the _____.

   _____
   _____

6. We can't allow our _____ to be appraised at a value lower than market value.

   _____
   _____

7. We have to respect everyone's _____ and _____.

   _____
   _____

8. The Jewel of Power is yours _____ to decide over your _____, _____, _____ and to do the things that need to be done.

CHAPTER 11: JEWEL OF POWER

_____

_____

The jewel of Power contributes to your _____ and _____. This will impact your promise.

_____

_____

CHAPTER 12: *JEWEL OF POSSIBILITIES*

I. **Opal will inspire_____, boost creativity it has dynamic energy, intensity, enhances competency and efficiency.**

    _____

    _____

    1. _____: a chance that something might exist happen or be true; the state or fact of being possible; something that might be done or might happen; something that is possible; abilities or qualities that could make someone or something better in the future.

        _____

        _____

II. **In Proverb 18:16, "A man's gift will make room for him, and bring him before great men."**

    1. We don't know who is watching our work.

        _____

        _____

    2. Walk in your own uniqueness.

        _____

        _____

CHAPTER 12: JEWEL OF POSSIBILITIES

  A. The worst thing we can do is steal someone's ideas and walk in an identity that is not ours.

  _____
  _____

  B. If we do not know our identity, we cannot be left with the matters of the whole world.

  _____
  _____

  C. We should not allow things to steal our possibilities of who God made and intended us to be.

  _____
  _____

  D. People with an identity crisis are the ones who cause the most chaos.

  _____
  _____

III. **The Perils of identity _____.**

   There are costs associated with identity theft.

   1. Identity theft leaves our jewels _____.

   _____
   _____

   2. Identity theft will mislead us into thinking that we have the authentic Jewel when we only have replicas, because they are stolen and imitated.

   _____
   _____

CHAPTER 12: JEWEL OF POSSIBILITIES

3. If we walk in other woman's identity, we will have to keep changing things about our identity.

   _____

   _____

IV. Learn how to _____ your own _____.

When God has given something to us, He gave it to us so that we can develop it, and all will see how great our God is.

1. When our mind begins to comprehend the possibilities of what we have, we will begin to see with supernatural eyes.

   _____

   _____

2. We must seize the moments to be around intelligent people, and this is where our confidence will show us where we are.

   _____

   _____

3. Don't be closed off to Possibilities because of what happened in the past.

   _____

   _____

Shutting ourselves off to the promises of Possibilities will limit the extent of who we can be and who we can reach. Our goal is to allow the Jewel of Possibilities to be revealed.

CHOSEN JEWEL

Connect with
CAPRICE L. LYONS

A jewel, regardless of its origin and unique characteristics, has value. Just as each jewel in the world is different, so is each person. As women, each attribute that makes us different, makes us who we are and we should take pride in ourselves and our unique facial features, tone of voice, height, skin tone, hair texture, size, age, etc. We can be critical of ourselves and may even have a wish list of things that we would change if we could.

Available at

amazon.com   BARNES & NOBLE
                     www.bn.com

Follow Me @capricelyons f 🐦 📷 in

For more info, visit www.capricelyons.com

www.ingramcontent.com/pod-product-compliance
Lightning Source LLC
Chambersburg PA
CBHW080022130526
44591CB00036B/2580